T0149374

Empowered

to do Good

Empowered
to do Good

Through God's Renewing Love

Josephine Anweting Edet

iUniverse, Inc.
Bloomington

Empowered to do Good
Through God's Renewing Love

Copyright © 2012 by Josephine Anweting Edet.

All rights reserved. No part of this book may be used or reproduced by
any means, graphic, electronic, or mechanical, including photocopying,
recording, taping or by any information storage retrieval system
without the written permission of the publisher except in the case of
brief quotations embodied in critical articles and reviews.

iUniverse books may be ordered through booksellers or by
contacting:

iUniverse
1663 Liberty Drive
Bloomington, IN 47403
www.iuniverse.com
1-800-Authors (1-800-288-4677)

Because of the dynamic nature of the Internet, any web addresses or
links contained in this book may have changed since publication and
may no longer be valid. The views expressed in this work are solely
those of the author and do not necessarily reflect the views of the
publisher, and the publisher hereby disclaims any responsibility for
them.

Any people depicted in stock imagery provided by Thinkstock are
models, and such images are being used for illustrative purposes only.
Certain stock imagery © Thinkstock.

ISBN: 978-1-4759-2728-3 (sc)
ISBN: 978-1-4759-2727-6 (ebk)

Printed in the United States of America

iUniverse rev. date: 05/23/2012

To God be the Glory.

Introduction

"There is a time for everything and a season for every activity under heaven: a time to be born and a time to die; a time to plant and a time to uproot, a time to kill and a time to heal . . . a time to be silent and a time to speak, a time to love and a time to hate, a time for war and a time for peace. I have seen the burden God has laid on men. He has made everything beautiful in its time. He has also put eternity in the hearts of men yet they cannot fathom what God has done from the beginning to the end." (Eccl 3:1-11)

So, what time is this? What time are we in? The answer depends on one's situation and circumstance. People view things differently and they respond differently. Many will agree however, that it is a time to search our lives, our souls, our relationships, and our worth. What is important? Is it our work, our faith, or our relationship? Relationships with whom and for what purpose? There are too many questions and few answers. Let us be honest; many of us are tired of spinning our wheels and are already asking how long will we continue like this?

One thing I know, someone must have an answer and I am ready to find out. How about you? "If you are not 100% satisfied with the way you see your life, what changes are you willing to make? Change is difficult at times, but when your pain is greater than your excuses, you will make a change and many people have defined madness as "doing the same thing while expecting a different result." If we want a different result, we must do something different. God never intended for us to toil without an end. That was why he provided a rest for his people. There remain, then, a Sabbath-rest for the people of God; for anyone who enters God's rest also rests from his own work, just as God did from his. Let us therefore, make every effort to enter that rest so that no one will fall by following their own example of disobedience. For the word of God is living and active." (Heb 4:9-12).

We are given instructions or a road map to take us to out divine destinies but are we using it? Are we following it? Few have found it and are happy. Many are still searching. It is not how much money we have made that brings satisfaction. Many have to come to realize that even with lots of money and fame, they still yearn for more. "My soul finds rest in God alone." (Ps 62:1). It is only God's plan that will stand and so he says "work out your salvation with fear and trembling for it is God who works in you to will and to act according to his good purpose." (Phil 2:12-13). We are called to be children of God without fault in a crooked and depraved generation."

We are called to live in obedience to God's plan for our lives. It is easier said than done, right? I agree. But this is the only hope I seem to see, to trust in the word of God and to obey what it says. In here are simple keys to living a life that is richer in every way than we can imagine. Will you take a walk with me for a little while?

Ok, so why should we even bother? My take on that is you never know until you try. Look at what he says "Come near to God and he will come near to you." (Jas 4:8).

How? In what way? Have we been standing afar? You answer for yourself and I will answer for myself. What does God want from us? What is he asking f us? He is asking for our hearts, time, love, and obedience. Everything, because all that we have, we received from him in the first place. So, we can only give as he has given to us. But how willing are we to let go and to surrender control of "my time, my money, my heart, my love, my mind"? "Self and mine" are our greatest set-back in walking with the Lord. He says "deny yourself". "What do you mean?" You ask. Well, I mean consider what affects others besides you. The bible says "whoever wants to save his life will lose it, but whoever loses his life for me and for the gospel will save it" (Mk 8:3-5). We have been cheating ourselves out of so many blessings because of unbelief.

Let us hear what the Lord says, "See to it that you do not refuse him who speaks. If they did not escape when they refused him who warned them on earth, how much less will we, if we turn away from him who warns us from heaven?" (Heb 12:25).

The Lord is inviting us to the banquet of life but we claim to be too busy and refuse his invitation. Can you imagine someone refusing an invitation to a wonderful banquet at these difficult economic times? Even in some middle class homes, things are difficult because of the times. Meals have to be rationed and it is worse for those who were already jobless and homeless because the number of people ready to donate money has dwindled. Would you be excited to receive $1000 worth of coupons for your groceries every month? I sure would be excited. But nobody considers the invitation to a banquet of life. The eternal bridegroom is sending out invitations to many to attend a wedding feast with him but how many are ready to come? Some completely ignore and overlook it and prefer to pretend that there is nothing like that. Consider what he says in Lk 14:16-24. A certain man was preparing a great banquet, he sent his servant to tell those who had been invited, "Come for everything is now ready". But they all alike began to make excuses . . . "Not one of those men who were invited will get a taste of my banquet." And similarly he says "I am going there to prepare a place for you. If I go and prepare a place for you, I will come back and take you with me and you also may be where I am." (Jn 14:2-3). Today the Lord is still inviting us but we have all kinds of excuses and very many have no intention of honoring his invitation. What do we expect? He turns to those who were not even qualified and he makes them qualify as it is said "the first shall be last and the last be first".

"Therefore I urge you, prepare your minds for action; be self-controlled; set your hope fully on the grace to be given you when Jesus Christ is revealed." (1 Pt 1:13).

CHAPTER 1

Importance of Decision

Everything begins with a decision. Things like what car to buy, house to build, where to live, what kind of job to do, school or church to attend, who to date or marry, and so on. Wherever we are in life or whatever job(s) we have, we are faced with a decision at one time or another. There are all kinds of decision-making ideas but most often, the first step is to recognize or identify the problem. Choices that we make in life depend on our decision. I need help here. What can we decide about our lives or existence? In other words, where did we come from and where are we going from here? Who are we? The bible tells us that we are children of God, made in his image and likeness but sometimes it is easy to forget and drift along in life. That can be very dangerous. We need to take time and ask ourselves some thought-provoking questions from time to time. Our society is very busy and that makes it hard to slow down. We need not wait till we are 77 years old and retired to find out why we are here. Some have retired at 40 or 50 years. It does not matter what age we prefer to retire. What matters is to slow down and take deliberate thought about our existence. Some have short and long term goals. It does not matter what you have if the Lord is not part of that process. Our maker and creator had a reason and a plan for our lives; which is to have a relationship with us. Many of us do not make time to allow that to happen. His heart is still the same, longing for us. With an everlasting love, he has cared for us unconditionally. When we were young children growing up, our parents made decisions for us about those things we needed. For instance, they made decisions about what clothes to buy for us, accommodation to live in, and places to go and so on. But there comes a time, when we grow up and we make our minds about what we want in life. At such times, the foundation on which we grew up can help our decision making process. We can head off to college, find a job, good man or woman to marry and start a family. We can bond with other Christians in a church and grow our faith and so on. But what happens when the foundation of our childhood was somewhat unstable? We can drift easily and make some not too good choices in life. What do we do then? Sometimes, it can be overwhelming especially when we have gone too far down the wrong end of the street to turn around and make a comeback. What we need more than anything else in such circumstances or situations is a realization that our own heavenly father has imprinted his stamp of ownership upon our lives. Once we turn it over to him, he can always make something beautiful out of it again. So, we are encouraged to bring our broken pieces of lives to Jesus. He said in Jl 2:25 that the years the locusts have eaten shall be restored. This is the message of mercy. God our father is so merciful. Once we have realized and decided that we need his help, he is eager and ready to help us out. That should be very comforting. That is the story of the prodigal son in Lk 15:11-24. He made it back to a loving and forgiving father and was restored. So, our God is ready to restore our brokenness.

From the beginning in Genesis, Adam was placed in the garden with a simple command "be fruitful and multiply, and replenish the earth and subdue it and have dominion over the fish of the sea, and over every living thing that moveth upon the earth" (Gn 1:28). What do you think of that command? Did he follow through with it? How about you and I? Have we considered what our parts should be in that command? Do I have a say here about our world today? What do you say about the world we are handing over to our children? Whose job is it to make this world a better place? Is it the president's job or that of congress and the law makers? Maybe it is the job of pastors and those in various levels of leadership. How about you? What part do you play in the big plan? There is a real danger in playing small and thinking it is none of your business. My son wrote a poem in 6th grade called "Tree".

"A tree is what I would be,
So big, strong and confident.
Trees can grow lots of leaves,
And I don't ever grow cold.
When it rains, I'm taking a bath.
It wouldn't hurt to lose a limb.
After summer, the fall comes in. I love
the cool wind blowing.
The snow makes me lose my leaves.
Except for when they come and cut me
down . . .
Thump!"
By Michael Edet.

We owe it to our children to make a difference. To live a legacy that will outlast us. God has given us a command and we can count on him to see us through. He knew we could do it and that is why he gave it to us. The danger is thinking we can do it by our own strength. On our own, we can do nothing. God's grace is sufficient for us to start today.

We can take baby steps towards making a difference. He said in Lk 10:19 "Behold, I give unto you power to tread on serpents and scorpions and over all the power of the enemy and nothing shall by any means hurt you. If God be for us, who can be against us? He has the power and he has given it to us. It is now left for us to do something with all that power he has given us. We must start by changing our thoughts and perceptions of who we really are. "As a man thinketh in his heart, so is he."

Further down in Prv 18:1, it says "through desire a man, having separated himself, seeketh and intermeddleth with all wisdom". So if we desire to know more, God will; grant that to us. Let us pray that the Lord will deliver our feet from stumbling and that his light will shine upon us and lead us in the right way so that in all things, we will do his will.

He promised to be us and never forsake us. He has not asked us to do the impossible. God's commandment is not burdensome 1John 5:3 and when we depend on him, he will carry us through. The bible says "with God all things are possible". Even if our logical mind tells us it cannot be done, the love of God renews us and we can do it again. We can love again, forgive again, and give to worthy causes without becoming bankrupt. The steadfast love of the Lord never ceases but it is new every moment (Lam 3:23).

The blessings we are seeking in so many places can only be found in obeying God's word. There is no lack in this universe. Every time there is an obituary, it makes me wonder how many people took their money with them. If they did not take those billions with them, it is still here. We just need to activate our financial blessing by doing what is asked of us. He says "Give and it shall be given unto you."

Our human wisdom cannot accept that because there are lots of things we need to do with our money. God is asking us to trust him to take us to another level of the impossible; a level where giving opens the door to financial blessings. Abraham was asked to give the most prized possession he had, his only son Isaac. He had waited till he was a 100 years old to have this son; and now God wants him to sacrifice the boy. But he trusted God and knew he could do the impossible. Do we trust God; and to what extent?

Making spiritual decisions based on what our natural minds can analyze, goes contrary to God's principle. When we are in Christ, all things become new as in 2 Corinthians 5:17 "if any man is in Christ, he is a new creation, the old has gone, and the new has come". We were taught in regard to our former ways of life, to put off the old self . . . and be made new in the attitude of our minds (Eph 4:23-24).

In this new nature, the spirit of God dwells in us and enables us to think like Christ and we are able to keep in step with the spirit (Gal 5:25). God's promises stand true that he will not leave nor forsake us. We have God's backing that if we do these things, we will never fall and we will receive a rich welcome into the eternal kingdom of our lord and savior Jesus Christ (2 Pt 1:10 11).

God's grace is sufficient. His strength is made perfect in our weakness. We need to take our eyes of everything and focus them on the promises of God. When unanswered questions weigh down our minds, let us remember who God is. We cannot question his strength to deliver. Whether we are making enough money to take care of our needs or not, God is still God. I believe standing with him in every situation is far better than us depending on ourselves. He is the source of all goodness. He was the one who provided a ram caught in the thicket by the horns (Gn 22:13) so that Abraham would not sacrifice Isaac. It was he who fed 5000 men with 5 loaves of bread and 2 fishes, not to mention the women and children. They still had 12 baskets of leftover (Mk 6:41). It was he who made manna (waffles) fall from the heaven and brought quails driven by the wind without number so that the children of Israel could eat in the wilderness. Do we trust in our own strength or in God's supernatural ability? He is not a man that he should lie or a son of man that he should repent. What he says he will do, he will do.

Remember the story in the book of 2 Kgs Chapters 6:24 and 7:1-20 where God supernaturally provided for the children of Israel who had suffered a severe famine as a result of the oppression of their enemies? The city was shut in because it was besieged by the enemy. The famine was so severe that 2 women got into an agreement to eat their own sons (2 Kgs 6:26-29). They boiled and ate the first woman's son. The next day, when it was time to eat the second woman's son, she hid him. The king was so angry when the matter was brought before him and he was determined to kill the man of God for not bringing them help. But God, who is ever true, turned that famine around overnight and plundered the enemy by giving their fortunes to the children of Israel. It took 3 days to carry the bounty. The doubting officer, who did not believe the word of the prophet, about God supernaturally providing for his people, was killed in the stampede; the overflow of free food and wealth. The moral of the story is that we must trust God and his word above all that we can imagine or think. We must trust him above our circumstances and previous experiences. "He is able to accomplish infinitely more than we would ever dare to ask or hope" (Eph 3:20). He has promised that heaven and earth will pass away, but his word will stand forever (Mat 24:35, Is 40:8).

Let us not settle for lies of the enemy. We are victorious. Jesus conquered the grave and we can boldly tell the devil to go to hell where he belongs. We refuse to negotiate with the devil. We refuse to buy into his lies. He tricked Eve in the garden by asking her if God really said she should not eat of any of the trees in the garden. Eve fell for his tricks; but we overcome him by the blood of the lamb and the word of our testimonies (Rev). We stand on the word just like Jesus did and we tell the devil that it is written "not by power, not by might but by my spirit says the Lord." (Zach 4:6).

Let us find that place of strength in the word of God. In it, we find answers to our questions, a place of power, prayer, deliverance, breakthrough, and where a miracle is born. Fall on your knees and find that place. So many have found it; and they came away renewed, refreshed, strengthened and healed from their afflictions. Let Christ be our solid rock. This foundation cannot be shaken. Let Christ be your foundation (1Cor 3:11) and you will not lose what you have built. If we walk in obedience, God is faithful and does his part (Is 1:19, 2Jn 6, 1Pt 1:4).

Let God fix whatever is wrong. Let his love renew you in every way whether it is financially, spiritually or physically. Do not delay your blessing by holding on to the past wrongdoings. God is ready to double your payback for all your trouble. You may not know how to pray. Just talk to your friend, his name is Jesus. If you do not find it hard to call on your friend when you want to talk, you should not find it hard to call on Jesus. He wants to bless us and he says "behold I stand at the door and knock" (Rv 3:20).

CHAPTER 2

Discovering Your Greatness

Let us take a look at this as we strive to serve the lord because he called us to lose the chains of injustice and untie the cords of the yoke to set the oppressed free, share food with the hungry and provide the poor wanderer with shelter. When you see the naked, clothe him and to also not turn away from your own flesh and blood. Your light will break forth like the dawn, and your healing will quickly appear. Your righteousness will go before you and the glory of the Lord will be your rear guard. Then you will call and the Lord will answer. You will cry for help and he will say "Here am I". If you do away with the yoke of oppression, the pointing finger and malicious talk, and spend yourself on behalf of the hungry and satisfy the needs of the oppressed, your light will rise in the darkness and your night will become like the noonday. The Lord will guide you always. He will satisfy your needs in a sun-scorched land and will strengthen your frame . . . (Is 58:1-12).

We are now called to bloom right where we are. That was what Joseph did. Wherever he was, he always put in his best even as a shepherd, slave, and prisoner until he became the prime minister of Egypt. He was always trusting in the lord and walking in integrity.

There are certain things about true greatness. It does not depend on your education and academic qualifications, though that might contribute in some way. It does not depend on your location or where you were born because God can move you and relocate you. Joseph started out with very humble beginnings but his trust and loyalty to God took him to great heights. So did David. He went from being a shepherd boy to killing the giant and eventually becoming King because of knowing who was with him.

Our mindsets have a lot to do with how high we can rise in life. There were people who were never taught they could become great in life. And because they could not imagine it, they saw themselves as "nobodies". They thought their efforts did not matter. In their minds, they were already defeated by their circumstances. There is something we need to bear in mind: No matter the situation or affliction we are currently facing, time will fix it. "The race is not to the swift or the battle to the strong ... but time and chance happen to them all" (Eccl 9:11). Time heals every hurt, it restores every loss, and it opens more opportunities. We have to prepare for the opportunity we want by starting today; right now where we are. We must discover the greatness from within us. We must speak greatness into our lives and our situations starting today. The Lord knows what we are passing through every day and he will not abandon us. How do you see yourself?

There was a woman who had no reason to believe but she said "it is well". Her son had just died but she said "it is well" (2Kgs 4:26). What are you saying about your situation today because what you think about, you speak about "for out of the overflow of his heart, his mouth speaks" (Lk 6:45). What you speak about, you bring about. Remember "the tongue has the power of life and death and those who love it will eat its fruit"? (Prv 18:21). So you have to speak into existence what you want to see. If you want joy, keep saying "I have joy in Jesus' name". Though people talk down, talk yourself up and keep at it till you see the results you want. Resurrect dead dreams by what you speak and add your actions to that because "faith" without works is dead (Jas 2:26).

Take a step of faith like the prophet in 1Kgs 18:43-45. He did not see rain, but he kept speaking about it. He did not doubt that God was able to make it rain. When you doubt, you give the enemy a chance to steal your vision and dream. Is 61:9 says this about us "all who see them will acknowledge that they are a people the lord had blessed". Is your life blessed? Is your life a testimony? If not, why not? We must keep speaking what God is speaking about us. Our words and his words must line up. Did you know that your brain responds to what you say and begins to perform at that level? Make your mind your servant by training it to think differently. "Be transformed by the renewing of your mind. Then you will be able to test and approve what God's will is; his good, pleasing and perfect will" (Rom 12:2).

Start training your mind today to obey what you say. We tame animals by training them. So, why can we not train our own minds? When we develop the habit of saying positive things like "I am fearfully and wonderfully made" (Ps 139:14), the subconscious mind receives it, and begins to carry it out. God's love never ceases as it is said in Lam 3:22-23 and our renewal process never ends. Expand your mind; it can stretch as far as you want it to go. Imagination is the greatest asset we have. "What things so ever ye desire, when ye pray, believe that ye receive them and ye shall have them" (Mk 11:24). But keep reading the following verses because our God is just and he will grant our desires as we obey what he says. He will not just throw our desires from the sky while walk in disobedience and regard iniquity in our hearts.

So, imagine yourself debt free, happy, healthy and whole. Train your mind to perform at that level. I imagine myself making a lot of money to help the poor everywhere I go. God's spirit works with our spirit (Rom 8:16) and "testifies with our spirit". "In the same way, the spirit helps us in our weaknesses. We do not know what we ought to pray for but the spirit himself intercedes for us with groans that words cannot express. He who searches the heart knows the mind of the spirit because the spirit intercedes for the saints in accordance with God's will" (Rom 8:26-27).

If we have the spirit of God, where does lack and poverty come from? The root is in our thinking. God has so much in store for us. We must do it his way and not ours to receive them. He says in Jn 14:15-16, "if you love me, you will obey what I command and I will ask the father and he will give you another counselor to be with you forever, the spirit of the truth". Further in Jn 16:12, he says "when the spirit of truth comes, he will guide you into all truth". See how much God cares for us and wants to bless us? But we must do our part. We must desire what he desires for him to hear us. Part of our obedience is to love one another. How do we do this? We look for the weak among us, poor, and the helpless. He says "if a man shuts his ears to the cry of the poor, he too will cry and not be answered" (Prv 21:13). Prosperity through obedience to God's word is a possibility. For with him, all things are possible. Even non-Christians have been abundantly blessed as they love and care for others. God's law of giving to receive is no secret. We are to be wise; building our lives in his word. "Each one should be careful how he builds for there is no other foundation to be laid except that which is already laid, Jesus Christ" (1Cor 3:10-11). If we are building outside the light of the word of God, we are toiling in the dark; putting our hopes in the standards of this world. But if we ask the Holy Spirit to give us light and understanding, we will receive as it was in Gn 1:13 when God said "let there be light", there was light.

We must always remember that trials must come. Our works will be tested, that is why it is important to work now while we can. Listen to this; "do not deceive yourselves. If anyone . . . thinks he is wise by the standard of his age, he should become a fool, so that he may become wise. The wisdom of this world is foolishness in the sight if God" (1Cor 3:18-19). God did not spare his son. He freely gave him to us. Will he not also with him freely give us all things? (Rom 8:32).

"Therefore do not lose heart. Though outwardly we are wasting away, yet inwardly we are being renewed day by day. For our light and momentary troubles are achieving us an eternal glory far outweighs them all. So, we fix our eyes not on what is seen, but on what is unseen. For what is seen is temporary but what is unseen is eternal" (2Cor 4:16-18).

Let us therefore do good. This is the time to do good for "at one time we were foolish, disobedient, deceived and enslaved by all kinds of passion and pleasures. We lived in malice and envy, being hated and hating one another. But when the kindness and love of God our savior appeared, he saved us . . . through the washing of rebirth and renewal by the Holy Spirit, whom he poured out on us generously through Jesus Christ our savior, so that having being justified by his grace, we might become heirs having the hope of eternal life" (Ti 3:3-7). This is true greatness. To be one with the Lord, so nothing can keep us bound. God's power in us can do tremendous things but we tend to play small. Do you not know that "you too are being built together to become a dwelling which God lives by his spirit"? (Eph 2:22)

"For we are God's workmanship, created in Christ Jesus to do good works which God prepared in advance for us" (Eph 2:10).

"Command those who are rich in this present world not to be arrogant and put their hopes in wealth, but instead in God who richly provides us with everything for our enjoyment. Command them to do good, be rich in good deeds, be generous, and willing to share. In this way, they will lay up treasure for themselves as a firm foundation for the coming age so that they may take hold of life that is truly life" (1Tim 6:17-19).

True greatness is in helping others. I remember vividly some blessing I received as a reward for giving. It was not money but way back when I was in high school. I had some classmates who always wanted me to help them with the lectures. This particular lesson was a bit difficult. It was about how kidneys produce urine. Remember, this was in high school (and I had no inkling in my mind that I was going to be a nurse when I grew up). The drawing was complicated, with the loop of Henle and those structures that make up a nephron. Well, I decided to help as much as I could from the drawing and lesson. I took the time and explained the process step by step. At the end, I realized I understood the lesson more by explaining it to others. That was a real eye-opener. There was another instance many years later when I was in my undergraduate nursing program. We were preparing for examinations in microbiology. I still had a lot to review for the exams and we were just a few hours away from starting the exams. That morning, one of my friends approached me to explain a few topics that she found challenging including different growth media, culture and so on. I had to suspend what I was reviewing to attend to her. In the process of explaining those topics to her, I gained more understanding. When we got into the exam hall, those topics were questions on the test and it was easy for me to answer them. I was so grateful I had taken the time to explain them to my friend. If I had not helped her, I would not have helped myself and done so well in that exam.

When you have a conviction in your spirit, hold on to it and believe it. When it is all said and done, God that will see us through to the end is our faith. We must have faith and confidence in him, trusting that our expectations shall come to pass. Mt 9:29 says "according to your faith will it be done to you" and Heb 10:35 says "do not throw away your confidence. It will be richly rewarded". So, whatever we believe, we must stand firm on it till the Lord perfects it. This involves waiting.

In this age of speed with microwaves and touch-button technology, it is hard to factor a "waiting period" into anything. God works according to his time and not ours. Let us learn from the farmers. They know that once a seed is planted, it takes it natural progression in the soil before we see the plant growing to bring forth fruit. This applies to our growth as well. Sometimes, we see an immediate result to prayers. At other times, there is a time of waiting and we must not give up. What should our attitude be when we are waiting? God knows best what is good for us and when to send it. There is a time for everything and God makes all things beautiful in his time. God sees the whole picture, but we see only in parts. Whatever we are waiting for? Let's follow Hb 2:2-3 that says "write down the revelation and make it plain on tablets so that a herald may run with it for it waits an appointed time. It speaks of the end and will not prove false. Though it linger, wait for it. It will certainly come and will not delay". Further in chapter 3 verses 17 and 18 it says "though the fig trees does not bud and there are no grapes on the vine, though the olive crop fails and the fields produce no food, though there are no sheep in the pen and no cattle in the stalls, yet I will rejoice in the Lord. I will be joyful in God my savior. Yes, we have to be joyful and we can only do it in the Lord". Let us pray: Dear Lord, help us have peace in our waiting. Let us not cast away our confidence in you. Amen.

CHAPTER 3

Overcoming Discouragement

Those who wait on the Lord will renew their strength (Is 40:31). When we turn on the radio and television, we can easily be discouraged by the pain and hopelessness that we see. Like the children in Haiti and other parts of the world, we feel hopeless even as adults. Sometimes that feeling of hopelessness comes and goes. It may last longer than necessary and sometimes lead to despair. So, what do we do when we feel hopeless? We turn to friends and family. Some automatically turn to God, the source of all strength. That occurs only when the individual already has some knowledge of the power of God. Those who lack this knowledge rely on friends and family. What if they have no friends and no family? The children in Haiti may not have friends and family considering the magnitude of the devastation that struck their capital city. Some lost both parents and all their siblings and are left all alone in this world at the mercy of well-wishers. I was listening to a 16 year old girl over the radio that had lost both parents, siblings and had nowhere to go. She slept in the streets. Can you imagine waking up to the hopelessness with no place to go and no one to turn to for a meal? In some parts of the world, people have so much to eat that they leave food to go bad in the refrigerators and kitchen tops. They throw old shoes away and old clothes that were fairly worn. I know some people cannot imagine it. Let us be a blessing to the people suffering in our world. Someone could be immensely blessed making good use of the things we take for granted. But first, we have to get to that place of thinking of those who are less fortunate than we are. Phil 2:4 says "each of you should look not only to your own interests, but also to the interests of others".

Our world is becoming really small compared to what we thought hundreds of years ago. Now people can fly all around the globe and we can hear news and political happenings far away. We watch scary news reports from third world countries as though they are another planet. There is no scarcity of news on Facebook, Twitter, MySpace, and all other kinds of networking tools.

My heart's yearning is to see children have a chance to make it through life. They need education, healthcare, good homes, a place to grow, and be loved. They are also vulnerable. They become targets for selfish gains, abuse and trafficking. God put his love in our hearts to share with those who need love. Let us love the children of the world so they can grow to become agents of change in this world. There is a place I know where pagans still practice child sacrificing. The children are considered evil if the mothers die during childbirth or if they give birth to more than one baby from a single pregnancy. If she has twins or triplets, the babies are sacrificed. If she dies after the birth of the baby, it is buried with her to prevent evil spirits from destroying the community.

Christ first loved us and gave himself for us (Eph 5:2). We are called to bear each other's burden. My humble prayer is that my life will make a difference for someone. I feel an obligation to contribute in some way. We have a part to play in making this world better. Sometimes, when we live far away from poverty, we tend to forget that half-a-world away people are dying from preventable things like hunger and thirst. Preventable diseases claim more lives in developing countries. I lost a sister-in-law to placenta previa which could have been managed differently. The hospital could not even perform a C-section to save her or the baby. The full-term baby girl died and so did the mother after she lost all her blood. God requires us to feel for others but sometimes we become discouraged. I grew up seeing a lot of poverty and suffering and I know first-hand that there are a lot of people out there who need help. My prayer is that the Lord will provide the resources to make those lives better. He is waiting for us to be his hands and feet. We can make someone's life better. We can relieve someone's suffering, place food on someone's table, pay for someone's tuition, and send the love of God into someone's heart through our efforts.

When we are burdened down and overwhelmed, let us turn to the Lord for courage. It is God's renewing power that empowers us lifting us out of despair. So, is it okay to become discouraged? Yes, is my answer. Even Elijah, God's mighty prophet who called down fire from heaven became discouraged. He said, "I have had enough, Lord". "Take my life. I am no better than my ancestors" (1kgs 19:4). After that, he lay down to sleep under the tree but the angel of the Lord woke him up to eat and drink and he was strengthened. Are you going through something overwhelming right now? We all have at one point or another. We can say "praise be to the God and father of our Lord Jesus Christ. The father of compassion and God of all comfort, who comforts us in all our troubles, so that we can comfort those in any trouble with the comfort we have received from him. For just as the sufferings of Christ flow over into our lives, so also through Christ our comfort overflows" (2Cor 1:3-5).

"Even youths grow tired and weary and young men stumble and fall; but those who hope in the Lord will renew their strength." When we look up to the Lord, he reaches out to us as in Is 41:10, "I will strengthen you and help you. I will uphold you with my righteous right hand". When your knees are weak from fear and anxiety sets in, say what the bible says "Let the weak say I am strong" (Joel3:10). Rather than wait for someone to encourage us in our down moment, let us encourage ourselves in the Lord like David did. Our strength comes from inside. It comes from the Lord. He gives us the ability to bounce back. David encouraged himself in the Lord when he lost everything to his enemy including his wives and children. (1Sm 30:6). He cried, wept, was broken hearted, and so were the men with him. He sought the Lord and he answered him. He asked for guidance and was able to pursue, overtake, and recover all that the enemy had stolen. Praise God! That should be our example. Let us not give into defeat. Mediocrity is not okay. Something must change. We cannot sit around and have a pity-party. Cry and weep if you may, but you must regain your strength in the Lord. "Weeping may endure for a night but joy cometh in the morning" (Ps 30:5). People will fail us, friends may let us down, jobs may disappear but God's love endures. That is why the bible says over and over "trust in the Lord". "Trust in him at all times O people; pour out your hearts to him for God is our refuge. Low born men are but a breath, the high born are but a lie, if weighed in a balance, they are nothing . . ." (Ps 62:8-9). Stay strong and connected through the word of God. Find a church group, find a prayer line, and get help! Do not go alone when you are in a storm. Learn to release it to the Lord through prayer and verbalization. Speak the word over your life and circumstance. Say what God says about you. I am an overcomer; you are an overcomer, claim victory in the name of Jesus. It takes practice but you can turn it around. Rom 8 from verse 31 say "if God be for us, who can be against us?" Verse 37, "in all these things, we are more than conquerors". Next verse "nothing can separate us from the love of God that is in Christ Jesus our Lord". We are powerful and we have the spirit of power. "But we have this treasure in jars of clay to show that this all-surpassing power is from God and not from us. We are hard pressed on every side, but not crushed, perplexed but not in despair; persecuted, but not abandoned, struck down, but not destroyed" (2Cor 4:7-9).

God alone can sustain us. So when we are down to nothing, let us remember that God is always up to something. "God is our refuge and strength, an ever-present help in trouble. Therefore we will not fear through the earth give away and the mountains fall into the heart of the sea."

Lay your foundation early before you get into a crisis because when you are already in the storm, that anchor of faith can hold you. Whatever we are going through will pass because nothing lasts forever. God's love alone endures forever. If we are around long enough, we will find out that time changes everything. There were times we thought we could not go through one more day. We thought we could not take one more step in our painful shoes. Praise God for we are still here. We are overcomers. We have to learn to overcome but it starts from the mind. There is more to us than what meets the eye! We are not grasshoppers. How do you see yourself? The children of Israel had sent out some spies to the land the Lord had promised them. They brought back the report that they saw themselves as grasshoppers compared to the people in the Land (Nm 13:33). So, what have you been saying to yourself about yourself? Have you forgotten who your God is? They forgot who had saved them from their enemies in the past. Only 2 men out of the 12 gave a favorable report. The Lord punished the other 10 and those who believed their bad report. So, whose report do you believe?

Change your self-talk. Speak positive, encouraging words to yourself. Start creating what you want by what you say. Your tongue carries creative power. Use it to your advantage. Ps 23:14 says "even though I walk through the valley of the shadow of death, I will fear no evil for you are with me". The Lord is right there with you where you are. He was with the three Hebrews in the fiery furnace (Dn 3:25). He was with Daniel in the Lion's den (Dn 6:22). I do not care what the situation may be. Say to yourself, "the Lord is my light and my salvation, whom shall I fear?"(Ps 27:1). Develop your own "do it yourself" manual for every situation you are facing now or in the future. The Holy Spirit is our teacher and counselor. He will instruct our hearts in what is right. Let us not forget that Jesus paid the full price for us not to lose our minds over stuff. He nailed the power of stuff on the cross so that stuff will no longer have power over us. Stuff will no longer have power over my ability to make good decisions. I say to myself that I am able to do all things through Christ who gives me strength (Phil 4:13). Not some things but "all things". I say I am blessed and highly favored because I know this is how God sees me. I am the apple of his eyes. I will keep speaking favor over my life until the things that I do not see begin to appear. I see with the eyes of faith for I walk by faith and not by sight. Though all around me is confusion and chaos, I choose to speak peace to myself. Peace be still. Even if it does not make sense, my bank account is empty, there is no gas in my car, my marriage is spinning, peace be still. Jesus was sleeping even though there was a storm (Lk 8:22-25). I receive anointing to sleep even when there is a storm in my life.

To walk in peace, learn to forgive those who have hurt you, stolen your money, identity, and rights. If you do not forgive, you will be greatly hindered form receiving peace. I will do something about the storms I can fix. If I am unable to fix them, I will release to the Lord and let him vindicate me. I will let him have them so that I can walk in peace. Is it easy? No, no, no! I will instead ask the Lord for grace as he promised that his "grace is sufficient" (2Cor 12:9).

You do not want to hold all that stuff in. There is something called "psychosomatic illness". It has to do with what your mind can do to your body. Talk about headaches, migraines, peptic ulcer, high blood pressure, panic attacks, loss of appetite, and more. You do not want that. Pray for the Lord's grace to forgive anyone who has caused you pain. Pray to receive peace, even if it is just peace with yourself. Be at peace with yourself and learn to let the Holy Spirit rule your heart. Start taking baby steps toward forgiveness. There is no true peace in stuff. Neither is there in wealth, drugs, controlling, and manipulating others. Let God get behind the wheel in that situation. Learn to lean not on your own understanding. Yes, we want to analyze it. Ps 119:165 says "great peace has they who love your law, and nothing can make them stumble".

"Trust in the Lord with all your heart and lean not on your own understanding . . . will bring health to your body and nourishment to your bones" (Prv 3:5-8).

We must draw close to the Lord. Only then will we discover how great we are. We overcome by the blood of the lamb and the word.

Greater is he that is in us than he that is in our world (1Jn 4:4). God is greater than our pain, needs, and uncertainties. We must all walk in his way and do his bidding. And as he promised when he was lifted up, he will draw all of us to himself.

If we really knew him, we would not delay one day without total surrender to him. What we seem to know is nothing compared to who he really is. Our understanding will be opened when we yearn to have a deeper relationship with him. "You will seek me and find me when you do so with all your heart" (Jer 29:13). Our lives will become an adventure when we walk with the Lord for he promised no good thing will be withheld from those who trust him. As we take baby steps into the unknown future, we will come to realize the true joy and peace that the world cannot give. "Remain in me and I will remain in you . . . If a man remains in me and I in him, he will bear much fruit; apart from me you can do nothing" (Jn 15:4-5).

CHAPTER 4

Your Citizenship Rights

What are your rights? Have they been granted? Did you demand that they be granted? In Acts 22:25, Paul was going to be flogged. He was going to be treated as a criminal. When the commissioner/commander found out that he was a Roman citizen, he became frightened. Further down in verse 29 of that same chapter, it says that those who were going to question Paul withdrew immediately. How about you and I? What rights have we forfeited as citizens of heaven where God is the King of the whole universe and Jesus our brother is seated at the right hand of our father as the high priest and commissioner?

They that know their rights as citizens of heaven (Phil 3:20) can boldly stand up against Satan the usurper. He is fake, powerless and intimidates through fear. Once he has gained entry through fear, he proceeds to cloud our minds with doubt till we can no longer focus on our rights. We have breaking news for Satan. His time is up and we know our rights. Our citizenship is in heaven where Christ is seated far above the principalities and powers. We claim our rights to good health, joy, love, peace, and all the great promises in the word of God.

3 John 2 says "beloved, I wish above all else that you might prosper and be in good health even as your soul prospers".

We must feed on the word of God. We have received the spirit of God and not the spirit of the world but the spirit that is from God that we may understand what God has freely given us. This is what we speak not in words taught by human wisdom but in words taught by the spirit expressing spiritual truth in spiritual words. "The man without the spirit does not accept the things that come from the spirit of God for they are foolishness to him and he cannot understand them because they are spiritually discerned" (1Cor 2:12-14). We do not depend on our own wisdom but on God's wisdom "for the foolishness of God is wiser than man's wisdom and the weakness of God is stronger than man's strength". Once we rely on God's wisdom, he gives us grace and strength.

Have you thought about the GPS (Global Positioning System) in automobiles? We rely on it to take us anywhere we want to go. That is a real wonder, right? We get in the car and drive miles and miles across the state by simply following the directions shown by the GPS. How about using a spiritual GPS which God has given us to guide us through this life to meet our Lord in eternity? God has a good plan for our lives and he reveals it in his word. While we are on this journey called life, we can only find the way when we follow his directions. Ps 119:34-36 says "give me understanding . . .direct me in the path of your commands . . . preserve my life according to your word . . ." We need directions because no one wants to stumble in the dark. Verse 165 of that psalm says "great peace has they who love your law, and nothing can make them stumble".

What we do with our lives depend on the choices we have made. For me, I choose to follow the bible. In fact, I am sold out and by the mercies of God, we will stand. When we doubt God's promises, we open the door for fear to enter and we begin to question the truth of who God says he is and what he can do. We are afraid of the future for we do not know what it will bring and we rationalize how the bills will be paid and how we cannot afford to give to the church or those in need. We forget God's promise in Ps 37:4 which says "delight thy self in the Lord and he will give thee the desires of the heart". When we delight ourselves in doing what he says, he will keep his promise. "Seek ye first the kingdom of God and his righteousness and all these things shall be added unto you" (Mt 6:33). Whether we need financial blessing or peace, joy or good health, he will give us once we walk in obedience to his commands. Most times, we ignore or fail to heed his word because the word has not taken root in our lives. Jas 1:6 says "He who doubts is like the wave of the sea, blown and tossed by the wind". Often times, we are afraid to give our hearts or whatever else it is we own because it makes us vulnerable. But fear is false evidence appearing real. I kept avoiding mammograms because of all the horrible stories I had heard about the pain. I finally summoned the courage to try after about 3 years only to find out that it was not that horrible.

Psalm 37:25 says "I have been young and now I'm old but I have neither seen the righteous forsaken nor their seeds begging for bread". God will not forsake us. Saint Paul said "I have learned the secret of being content in any and every situation, whether well fed, hungry, living in plenty or in want. I can do everything through him who gives me strength" (Phil4:12-13).

Acts of love and kindness break the power of darkness. They allow God's radiant light to shine into our lives so that we can see clearly the path he has set before us.

Psalm 90:12, "teach us to number our days aright that we may gain a heart of wisdom".

Ps 50:9-12, "I have no need for a bull from your stall or of goats from your pens, for every animal in the forest is mine and the cattle on a thousand hills . . . if I were hungry, I would not tell you for the world is mine and all that is in it".

So why are we afraid to trust God with the little that we have? All he wants to do is bless us. He takes what we give him, blesses, multiplies and sends it back to us in multiples. On the other hand, our enemy the devil is working overtime to trick us out of this blessing.

In the natural, we take care to nourish and keep our bodies well fed and looking good but we fail to nourish our spirit which is made in the image of God. "God is a spirit and his worshippers must worship in spirit and truth" (Jn 4:24). Success in our lives is very possible when we have made up our minds to trust God totally. We must allow our spirit to grow as we feed on the word of God. Our obedience will be complete and we will be able to live based on God's blue print.

If only we could slow down and discover the great promises in the word. The world will not burn down if we slow down. In fact, it will simply continue as usual. Our wonderful employers will barely miss us when we are gone. My conclusion? Slow down and make time for the things that really matter; more of Jesus, less of me.

"God's divine power has given us everything that we need for life and godliness through our knowledge of him who called us by his glory and goodness. He has given us his great and precious promises so that through them, we may participate in the divine nature and escape the corruption in this world caused by evil desires" (2Pt 1:3-4). What price did you pay for your citizenship?

We are called to be imitators of Christ. We have received a lot from him. What are we willing to give? A beautiful story was told about people who gave back because of the love they received from Jesus. The woman in Lk 7:31-50 brought her an alabaster jar of perfume and poured it over Jesus' feet. It was an expensive perfume. To her, it was nothing compared to the love, healing and forgiveness she had received.

When Zacchaeus encountered Jesus, he made up his mind to pay back four times the amount of anything he had cheated from anybody (Lk 19:8). All through the bible, people were changed after they had an encounter with Jesus. The demon-possessed man in Lk 8:27-39 "from whom the demons had gone out begged to go with him, but Jesus sent him away . . . so the man went away and told all over town how much Jesus had done for him." We encounter the Holy Spirit every day. How has that changed us? How has it changed our perception of others and our outlook on life? What have we done differently since our encounter with Jesus?

My high school principal always told us that "by their fruits you shall know them". I thought it was just her way of driving home her point as she spoke to us, but as I studied the bible, I came across Lk 6:43-45 which says "no good tree bears bad fruit and no bad tree bears good fruit. Each tree is recognized by its own fruit. People do not pick figs from thorn bushes or grapes from briers. The good man brings good things out of the good stored in his heart and the evil man brings out evil things out of the evil stored in his heart. For out of the overflow of his heart, his mouth speaks".

We must let the renewing power of God's love empower us to bear good fruit that will bring others to the saving knowledge of Christ. Good deeds break barriers. What good deeds are we willing to give to the service of God and others? What talents and treasures are we willing to share with the world? Let us be "to God aroma of Christ among" the people we meet every day (2Cor 2:15). Is 7:9 says "if you do not stand firm in your faith, you will not stand at all". We have freely received everything from the Lord and we must be willing to give just as we received. "Don't be deceived my dear brothers. Every good and perfect gift is from above, coming down from the father of the heavenly lights, who does not change like shifting shadows. He chose to give us birth through the word of truth that we might be a kind of first fruits of all he created" (Jas 1:17-18). "Our God will uphold us as we have faith in him" (2Chr 20:20).

Our warfare with unprofitable hard work will surely come to an end in his time. Our God will bring an end to poverty in our lives if we faint not in doing good. He will grant all that our hearts desire. Let us resolve not to let the enemy steal from us anymore. We will walk in total obedience to the word of truth that is able to set us free. Freedom is our citizenship right. Free from the oppression of sin and Satan.

CHAPTER 5

Unlock Your Treasure Chest

"Wisdom is more precious than rubies, and nothing you desire can compare with her" (Prv 8:11).

"Blessed is the man who finds wisdom, the man who gains understanding, for she is more profitable than silver and yields better returns than gold" (Prv 3: 13-14).

"Submit to God. Be at peace with him. In this way, prosperity will come to you. Accept instructions from him mouth and lay up his words in your heart . . . then the almighty will be your gold, the choicest silver for you" (Jb 22:21-25).

"You will eat the fruit of your labor. Blessings and prosperity will be yours." "Blessed are all who fear the Lord, who walk in his ways" (Ps 128:1-2).

There is nothing wrong with getting blessed. I do not know about you but I am ready to receive all the blessings that God has stored for me. This is the reason obedience is a key to receiving whatever I need. How about you? He commanded Joshua and today he is commanding us. "Do not let this book of the law depart from your mouth. Meditate on it day and night so that you may be careful to do everything written in it. Then you will be prosperous and successful. Have I not commanded you? Be strong and courageous. Do not be terrified. Do not be discouraged, for the Lord your God will be with you wherever you go" (Jos 1:8-9).

Also it says in 1Cor 2:9 that no eye has seen, no ear has heard, no mind has conceived what God has prepared for those who love him. It is only revealed by the spirit and word of God. "Study to shew thyself approved not to be ashamed, rightly dividing the word of truth" (2Tm 2:15).

Are you walking alone in this journey of life without the light of God to guide you? By our strength alone, we cannot prevail. Even "though I walk through the valley of the shadow of death, I will fear no evil for thou art with me" (Ps 23:4). When I know the Lord sees the future that I cannot see, it gives me great peace. Our future is secure only in him and he is more powerful than everything that had held me down. I am ready in the name of Jesus to come out of whatever stronghold held me down. I am taking my blessing back as I walk in obedience to God's word. We are called to obey even though we cannot understand how the Lord will do it. We still believe and try to pursue his plans to bless us. We will not let pain or doubt or forgiveness keep us out of our blessing. Let us make up our minds to get out of captivity into our promised land.

Abraham obeyed God and in the book of Genesis 22: 15-18, the Lord says "because you have done this . . . I will surely bless you and make your descendants as numerous as the stars in the sky and as the sand on the seashore. Your descendants will take possession of the cities of their enemies. And through your offspring, all nations on earth will be blessed because you have obeyed me".

When we obey the Lord and follow his instructions, his precepts will guide us step by step into our destiny.

Our enemy the devil is defeated because God gave us victory on the cross. Jesus paid the price for us and now he is seated in the heavenlies far above principalities and powers (Eph 1:21). He paid for my health, spiritual wellbeing, financial prosperity and total restoration for my children and their children. He paid once and for all. If we do not claim our blessings we only have ourselves to blame. I do not know about you but the blessings of Abraham are mine and the word of God is the key to unlock the treasures that have been stored for me. I am going to the next level. Will you journey with me to the level of abundant blessings? How will we do this? By seeking first the kingdom of God so that all the blessings will be added to us according to his promises (Lk 12:31). He who promised us is faithful. For God does not lie. What he says, he will do (Nm 23:19). Our real enemy is a liar, thief and wants to rob us of our blessings through disobedience. Resist him and stand in faith because disobedience is a serious matter with God. Remember what he said in 1Sam 22 when Saul disobeyed the instructions of Samuel the prophet? "Obedience is better than sacrifice." Those who disobeyed Moses never entered the Promised Land.

In his time, God is able to make all things beautiful. In the book of Ezekiel, the valley was full of dry bones. When God commanded breath upon them, they stood up as a mighty army. No one knows the mind of God. Our part is to obey and God will do the rest. I am all for finding out the great treasure God has for me. So, I will continue this race by his grace and not look back because "no one who puts his hand to the plow and looks back is fit for service in the kingdom of God" (Luke 9:62). I do not know what area of your life is experiencing dryness but I believe that every dry area of my life will come back to life in Jesus' name. There is a great price and a crown; a reward of faithfulness that awaits us at the end of our journey. God will perfect all that concerns us. If he could feed 600,000 men in the wilderness with meat for a whole month, he can feed, clothe and take care of my needs once I walk in obedience. "Abram believed the Lord and it was credited to him as righteousness" (Gn 15:16). I refuse to lean on my own understandings. If we let the devil beat us down with woes, discouragement, lack and poverty, what shall we say about the blood of Jesus? He died to set us free in every area! Listen to what the Lord says about obedience in financial matters. If we cannot be trusted with very little riches, then how can we be trusted with much? If we cannot be trusted with the riches of this world, then who will entrust us the real treasures of heaven? If we are not faithful in little, how will we be faithful in much? (LK 16:10-12). Faithfulness in little things always leads to great blessings. We shall not despise the days of small beginnings. The race of this life is not to the swift and the battle is not to the strong but chance and time will happen to them (Eccl 9:11).

God in his goodness has not asked us to do the impossible. If we abide in the lord and his word abides in us, we can do all that he has commanded (Jn 15:5). We must die to our own reasoning. We must die to the world's views concerning spiritual matters. Unless a grain of wheat falls to the ground and dies, it cannot produce much. When it dies, it brings forth much fruit (Jn 12:24). We must in the same way die so that we can bear much fruit for the Lord. In this time and chance that happens to all flesh, we eagerly await God's invitation. We die to our natural understanding and we live only trusting him. There are so many worries and uncertainties regarding the future but if we learn to give it all to the Lord, we can bear our burdens with gladness in the knowledge of the fact that we are not alone. Phil 4:13 says that we can do all things through Christ who strengthens us. Note that it says "all things" not "some things". "All things" include forgiving our enemies, letting go of the past, loving those who do not deserve to be loved and living a triumphant life. We can do all these things and more through the Holy Spirit that lives within us. This is where our child-like faith comes in. Insisting on doing things our own way and depending on our own strength will only make the journey difficult. Children forgive easily and they have a lot of trust. I remember many times when I rushed to separate my children thinking they were fighting only to watch them reconcile as though nothing had occurred. In a few minutes, they were best friends again and I wondered why I ever got myself worked-up in the first place. The bible says unless we change and become like little children, we cannot inherit the kingdom of heaven (Mt 18:3). As we get older, we process things differently and this gets more difficult. We analyzed situations and create more files in our heads for every hurt and unkind word ever spoken to us. With time, we will have more files than a computer of things that were done to us and of people we never want to talk to again and so on. Even in the church, we have those on our list. While having fellowship with God and other believers, there are those we do not want to sit next to because they had stepped on our pretty toes. It is interesting to note that as we go through life, people will hurt us whether they mean it or not. Jesus gave us an example. He washed Judas' stinking feet (ouch!) even though he knew fully well that with those feet, Judas was going to lead the way for the people who would arrest and crucify him. I would have personally excluded Judas from the dinner but Jesus treated him no differently from the others. Listen to what he says in Phil 2:5-11, "your attitude should be the same as that of Jesus Christ: who being in a very nature God, did not consider equality with God as something to be grasped. Instead, he made himself nothing; taking the very nature of a servant being made in human likeness . . ." He became a God-servant or King-servant. He was God and King but became a servant when they pulled his beard, spat on him, slapped him in the face and jeered at him. He did not revile back. He held his peace and asked the father to forgive them. Have we tried anything close to that? When we are wrongly treated for being Christians? How did we respond?

Let us continue to work out our salvation with fear and trembling for it is God who works in us to will and do his good pleasure. The promise of God stands sure that we have received the spirit of power, love, a sound mind and not a spirit of fear (1Tm 1:7). The spirit of fear is a terrible thing. Fear has gotten many people into terrible mistakes. We are anxious about the future. We are afraid of what will happen in years to come. For instance we are afraid about whether or not we will have a retirement plan or if our children will be able to go to school. We have not even seen tomorrow and yet we worry about things we cannot control. I know I worry a lot but I have come to realize that there are things I have no control over. For instance, I cannot control what people may say about me, but I can control my reaction. The same thing applies to my resources. I can give as I have been given. I have a free will to donate to charity because God has graciously blessed me not because of my goodness but because of his mercy. God gave his love so I can give love in return. He gave financial increase, joy and more so that we can also give. When hurtful words are spoken, we release them to the Lord and ask the Holy Spirit to give us peace. We can mature to a place where we can forgive and share our love genuinely with others. We give part of what we have received because we cannot give what we do not have. We are called to fight the good fight of faith (1 Tm 6:12). Our faith is the only thing that is worth fighting for because even the rich in this world are reminded to store up treasures for themselves in heaven and to take hold of that which is truly life. God's love alone renews us to be like him.

Spiritual maturity takes time and training. We are to renew and re-train our minds. We are to be faithful stewards of what God has given us. As we become faithful in little, he can trust us with more. Then he makes us faithful in more.

You know, I love to share my testimonies of God's goodness. I learned to make donuts, buns and hush puppies by stumbling on the recipe in the kitchen. Friends and customers often tell me that it tasted better than the ones they have tried before and I am always quick to say that I give God the glory because the Holy Spirit gave me the recipe. This makes a lot of people uncomfortable but I explain that I had been searching for this recipe for a long time and had been asking friends to teach me with no luck. On a certain day when I slowed down long enough, I found the recipe in my kitchen and it turned out to be better than I would have imagined. So, I give God the credit. I wonder why people are uncomfortable to talk about what God can do. He can raise the dead to life, he can teach me and you all what we need to know by his spirit (Jas 1:5). I am not ashamed to say that if it were not for the Lord who rescued me from a certain way of life, I would have gone down the wrong end of the street a long time ago. Now, I know my redeemer lives and he is able to keep me to the end. So, what are you boasting about today? Do not be ashamed to share your testimonies of what God has done. Remember he says in Mk 8:38 that "if anyone is ashamed of me and my words in this adulterous and sinful generation, the son of man will be ashamed of him when he comes in his father's glory with the angels".

All that we have, we received from God. It is said "freely you have received, freely you shall give". I remember many years ago when I was much younger, that there was a Teacher's Training College (TTC) near a place where I spent some holidays. I did not visit the college but could hear them sing when it was lunch time. That song got stuck in my memory because I would hear it every day. They sang "some have food but cannot eat. Some can eat but have no food. We have food and we can eat. Glory be to you, O Lord". It used to amuse me. I remember telling myself each time "they are singing that funny song". Now that I am older, I have come to realize that there is a lot of meaning to that song. It is God who gives as it is said in 2Cor 9:10-12, "he who supplies seed to the sower and bread for food will also supply and increase your store of seed and will enlarge the harvest of your righteousness. You will be made rich in every way so that you can be generous on every occasion and will result in thanksgiving to God. This service that you perform is not only supplying the needs of God's people but is also overflowing in many expressions of thanks to God".

This grace comes upon us to make us abound as givers who are always feeding and giving to somebody's need. God has called us to be administrators of his wealth. We have been made conduits of God's blessings. You can enrich the lives of suffering people oversees without leaving the comfort of your home unlike the missionaries of old who had to feel the discomfort and dangers of travelling abroad. Missionaries like Mary Slessor, took the good news of salvation to many who were in the dark bound by Satan's blindness to the light of God that was shining in other parts of the world. This dear lady spent her whole life saving babies from being sacrificed. She taught the word of God to the young, old and administered justice. We cannot understand all that these missionaries went through but they did it for the kingdom of God. Many lives were changed forever because of their sacrifices. There are so many things we do not understand but God has promised abundant blessings when we go the extra mile to help somebody along life's journey. As we take care of their needs, God takes care of our needs and makes his grace abound to us. This way, we never grow weary. And as we continue, we shall hear his welcoming words "well done thou good and faithful servant". I believe we will increase in many more ways than we can imagine and we answer that call to "let thy kingdom come on earth as it is in heaven". Let us go by faith trusting that our jug of oil shall not run dry but will be multiplied as it happened to the widow of Zeraphath after she fed the prophet of God (1Kgs 17:16). She thought in the severe famine that she and her son would starve to death after that last meal, but she obeyed the prophet and found out in her surprise that God was more than able to multiply her supply of food.

May the Lord increase us for every good work even in this economic meltdown so that we can obey his instructions. "Give and it shall be given unto you, good measure pressed down shaken together and running over" (Lk 6:38).

I refuse to let poverty into my spirit because Christ bore my poverty when he became a curse for me (Gal 3:13-14) that I may receive the blessing of Abraham. The bible says though Christ was rich, he took our poverty and became poor for our sake. I receive this blessing and walk in that liberty. As we give whatever we have, little be it or much, God will multiply it. We cannot understand how through our natural minds but as we let our minds be renewed through the word of God. He enlightens the eyes of our understanding. When we follow God's principle of living a blessed and abundant life, the curse of poverty will be broken from our lives. Let us kick our faith into high gear and break the backbone of poverty. I declare that God's grace is sufficient to help pay my bills. His grace grants me favor on every side. All my needs are supernaturally met as I align my giving with God's word.

This also applies to forgiveness because past offences can lead to bitterness. Bitterness will hinder the flow of God's blessings. God desires abundance for me and for you. He will make a river of life and health to flow from us. I am fearfully and wonderfully made and I refuse to settle for the lies of the devil. I speak forth what I desire because as a tither, God has promised to open the windows of heaven and pour out a blessing for me. Let us love in word and in deed because faith, hope and love will remain. And the greatest of these is love (1Cor 13:13). A dear Christian always says we should not be like the Dead Sea that always receives without giving out. When we love our fellow human beings, we are in the light. In 1John 3:17-20, it says "if anyone has material possessions and sees his brother in need but has no pity on him, how can the love of God be on him . . . Let us not love with words or tongue but with actions. This is how we know that we belong to the truth and set our hearts at rest in his presence . . . for God is greater than our hearts and he knows everything".

My prayer always is that the Lord will enlighten the eyes of our understanding so that we may know the hope to which we have been called, the riches to his glorious inheritance, and his incomparably great power that raised Jesus from the dead. Amen.

CHAPTER 6

I Refuse To Eat My Seed

As long as the earth remains, seed time and harvest time shall not cease so also cold and heat, summer and winter, and day and night shall not cease (Gen 8:22).

As we saw earlier, there has to be a planting seed to receive a harvest. "Unless a kernel of wheat falls to the ground and dies, it remains only a single seed; but if it dies, it produces many seeds" (Jn 12:24).

I am sure a lot of us have heard it over and over that it is more blessed to give than to receive. I know many of us do not take it seriously. We would rather hold onto what we have. I have decided to put it into practice by taking baby steps. I pray I will be around long enough to see what happens because I believe God will send a reward. There are a lot of things in our lives that we would rather just leave alone. I will practice giving so that I will receive more to the glory of God. There is a mystery about planting seeds even in the natural.

I personally love to dig in the dirt to plant in the back of the house. Each time I plant a seed, it becomes a plant and brings fruit with more seeds. It is hard work tilling in the dirt but when I see the tomatoes, pepper, cucumber and basil, I cannot help doing it again each year. I do not eat the tomato seeds but plant them instead to bring more fruits. If we are willing to do this in the natural, why not try the spiritual also? The spiritual realm governs the physical. When we obey the word of God, we activate the spiritual. I have told myself that I would rather be a fool in God's school than lean on my own understanding. The bible says "trust in the Lord with all thine heart and lean not on your own understanding". I may not have thousands of dollars to sow but I may have twenty or thirty. So I will start small and learn the discipline of giving because down the raod, it will bless somebody and return to me in different forms of blessings. I am standing on God's word that the more I give, the more I will receive. So, I am learning to give other things besides money. I give love to people who do not deserve it because Jesus has shown me love so many times even when I did things that were unlovable.

We are encouraged to be generous as we already are in so many things. "See that you excel in this grace of giving" (2Cor 8:7).

We can give hope, a smile, and encouragement. Giving is not limited to money so that those who do not have will not feel hard pressed. Let us infect our families and communities with gratitude. Let the people around you know how grateful you are to be a part of their lives. Give the gift of prayer. Pray for those who are bitter that God's love will flood their hearts with joy and peace. I pray that the Lord by his spirit will tear the veil of darkness that has kept us from giving and living the prosperous life.

There is this song that we used to sing in high school. I do not know the writer. It says

1). Oh scatter seeds of loving deeds
Along the fertile fields;
For grain will grow from what you sow,
And fruitful harvest yield.

Then day by day . . . along your
way . . .
The seeds of pro . . . mise cast . . .
That ripened grain . . . from hill and
plain . . .
Be gathered home . . . at last

2). Though sown in Tears through
weary years,
The seed will surely live
Though great the cost, it is not lost,
For God will fruitage give.

3). The harvest home of God will come
And after toil and care,
With joy untold, your sheaves of gold,
Will all be gathered there.

(From Sacred Songs and Solos)

Be blessed:

When we read Ps 112, it says "blessed be the man who fears the Lord, who finds great delight in His commands . . . His children will be mighty in the land . . . wealth and riches are in his house . . . Surely he will never be shaken . . . he has scattered abroad his gifts to the poor, his righteousness endures forever; his horn will be lifted in honor."

When Jesus asked a question about which was the greatest commandment, he said "love the Lord your God will all your soul, with all your might and with all your strength. The second is to love your neighbor as yourself". The bible further says that obeying these commandments is better than "all the burnt offering and sacrifices". The Lord himself said once we do this, we shall not be far from the kingdom of God (Mk 12:33-34).

Every promise of God is in the bible. We must walk in obedience to enjoy its riches. When we refuse to obey, we cannot receive the blessings. In the same gospel of Mk 4:24-25, it says "consider fully what you hear" because "with the measure you use, it will be measured to you and even more. Whoever has will be given more; whoever does not have, even what he has will be taken away".

When we hear the word and act on it, we begin to see results. Then the Lord gives us more words and results. Little by little, our lives begin to change, reflecting more the life of Christ until "it is no longer 1 that lives but Christ that lives in me." (Gal 2:20).

God's seed remains in those who walk in obedience. His seed in his word and the children of his carry the seed and they love one another. Listen to 1Pet: 22-23, "now that you have purified yourselves by obeying the truth so that you have sincere love for your brothers, love one another deeply from your heart. For you have been born again not of perishable seed, but of imperishable through the living and enduring word of God."

When we love in word and deed, we fulfill the word of God and he makes more blessings and grace abound towards us so that we can do more good works. "Everyone born of God overcomes the world" (1 John 5:4). He gives seed to the sower and bread to the eater and is able to meet all our needs. Whatever the Lord lays in my hand and puts in my heart should be to do his will. I am ready for a change and this business of giving, sowing seeds, and meeting the needs of others can start with even the smallest things we do for others. Seeds of good deeds could be as simple as giving a ride to someone who has no car, so he / she could get from point A to B. This carries a reward. It could be saying a kind word or giving someone an encouragement and when possible, we can also give money in a seed form to support God's kingdom on earth.

May the Lord enlighten the eyes of our understanding so that with his strength, we can stop the enemy from stealing from us. Now that the seed has landed on the fertile soil of our hearts, we pray that it will take root and bear fruits to the glory of God's name.

Stars Are Singing

Can you hear the children crying in the rubble?
Buried in the darkness with no hope of survival
We are fallen, paying the price for others
So the world will notice.

It has gone on too long, they looked away,
Turned their faces away,
They turned their hearts away and let the children
go astray.

Now they are buried in the rubble never to rise again
Paying the price for others that the world will notice.

Hearts are broken as the lives are broken
All of a sudden the buildings are falling
The children are calling as their lives have fallen
Hear the children crying, parents are dying buried
in the rubble.

Mercy is falling from the high and mighty
Sending all their armies through the valleys
Seeking the low and fallen buried in the rubble.

Limbs are broken, lives are broken
Mercy is falling from the high and mighty
Lives are rising once buried in the rubble
Hopes are rising for the sun is shining.

Bright stars are singing
Hollywood stars are singing
Across the horizon bright stars are shining
Lives are changing once dazed and broken
As the stars are shining across the horizon.

This is for the children of Haiti. Some were covered beneath the rubble of fallen buildings and buried alive never to rise again. Now, we have to stand up and help the children all over the world and make our world a better place.

Speak up and judge fairly, defend the rights of the poor and needy" (Prv 31:9). I pray that the blindfold from the enemy will be removed from our eyes that we may tap into his wonderful law of prosperity. Amen.

My Sample Prayer List

I speak forth the things that are not as though they be in Jesus' name.

I receive peace in all my endeavors in the Name of Jesus

I can do all things through Christ who strengthens me

I am blessed and highly favored in Jesus' name

My blessing are locating me now in Jesus' name

I am an overcomer; I will never give up in Jesus' name

I am on the Lord's side and the Lord is on my side

I am standing on Jesus the solid rock in Jesus' name

New doors and opportunities are opening up for me every day in Jesus' name

I soak my feet in the blood of Jesus and everywhere my feet touch, I claim for a possession in the name of Jesus.

My mind is renewed in Jesus' name

Holy Spirit changes my identity to Fire in Jesus name.

Holy Spirit of God, make me a terror unto my enemies in Jesus' name.

I am above and not beneath in the name of Jesus.

I receive the spirit of power, of love and a sound mind in Jesus' name

I will fulfill my destiny in Jesus' name.

I declare that my house is a house of prayer and no evil shall come near my dwelling in Jesus' name.

Whatever my hands find to do shall prosper in Jesus' name.

I received the wisdom of God to pursue and overtake in every area if my life in Jesus' name.

It is my time to shine in Jesus' name.

I come against the spirit of fear with the blood of Jesus

I receive the righteousness of Christ in Jesus' name.

Father, thank you for giving me the strength of high heaven today. I receive the mind of Christ. Amen